#Momspray

Copyright © 2021
#momspray (30 Days Prayer Guide for Mothers)
TINU KUTI

ISBN: 978-978-989-800-8

Published by:
T'omode Ltd.
13, Moshood Abiola Crescent, off Toyin street, Ikeja, Lagos, Nigeria.
atinukekuti@gmail.com, 08030588527

Layout/Design:
AyanfeOluwa Publishing Services (APS)

Printed by:
Greenlab Solutions,
Lagos Nigeria.

FOREWORD

While having a discussion with Pastor Tinu some years ago about raising our children the kingdom way, she mentioned Jochebed (Moses' mother). It was interesting to note that Jochebed's three children were leaders in Israel at the same time. More intriguing was how she managed to indoctrinate Moses in the few years he stayed with her, such that he didn't forget his roots and eventually became Israel's deliverer.

Though we didn't have full insight into Jochebed's methods that day, Pastor Tinu continued in her search for answers as to how to raise "change agents" in these times.

This book is definitely an answer and a very useful tool full of insights as to how to prayerfully raise our children in this challenging times.

Thank you Pastor Tinu for writing this insightful book. This prayer book is highly recommended to every parent who desires to raise their children as change agents and leaders in their generation.

Folake Daniels
March 2021 - Lagos, Nigeria.

FOREWORD

The challenges facing our children today are immense. Things are changing fast in the wrong direction and our children are being exposed to many negative and harmful influences like never before.

Many parents are overwhelmed and anxious, wondering what the future holds for their children and how they will turn out.

This book you have in your hands is just what is needed at this time. It's to the point, practical and easy to read.

It deals with the most powerful resource for raising children - prayer.

It's a guide to help you know what to pray for, how to pray and why.

The author herself has practiced the principles of this book and together with her husband has raised four amazing daughters.

I am confident that by reading this book and following its instructions you also will be able to bring significant change through prayer in the life of your children.

Pastor Sola Mabogunje
Lead Pastor, The Scent of Christ Church, Lagos.

DEDICATION

\#Momspray is dedicated to all the women in my life, starting with my two moms who taught me how to pray: Olufunke Ilori Okondo and Wuraola Olatundun Kuti (of blessed memory).

My Maternal Grand Mother, Princess Ibitayo Babajide (nee Adeyemi), who taught me the power of daily confession over my children.

My four beautiful angels, who for years patiently endured and are still enduring my long daily confession over them, whether physically or over the phone. I love you.

My Jochebed Mothers Circle, you rock! You are the motivation for this prayer book. Keep being intentional in raising your change agents. Your reward is sure. I appreciate you.

My husband Olufolajimi who supported me and is still supporting me tremendously through this motherhood journey. I salute and love you!

All my siblings and family members, thank you for all you do.

All who stand in the capacity of mentors to me, thank you for holding my hands at any point in time. I appreciate you.

All friends and well wishers, thank you for your support.

ACKNOWLEDGEMENT

give thanks and Glory to Almighty God for the Grace to put these prayers together into a book.

I want to acknowledge my Father - in - love, Archdeacon Olusegun Kuti, who helped with the theological and fine print editing of the book. I appreciate you Dad.

My gratitude also goes to my Brother - in - love, Olusola Kuti @Greenlab who worked hard to ensure I got copies ready for my book introduction. Thank you so much. I appreciate you.

Hello Moms! **#momspray** is a prayer movement for our change agents (our children). They are under siege by the world's culture and trends. The Lord impressed this prayer call on my heart in February of the year 2020, after I attended an annual ministers conference in Lagos, Nigeria. I left the conference recharged and immediately swung to put things in place. I made my intentions public to embark on a 30 days prayer journey to redeem our children from the darkness that seeks to envelop them, close to four hundred women enrolled online within two weeks. Little did I know that the entire world would experience a total lockdown halfway through the prayers, due to Covid -19 pandemic. Like Jochebed, we will not sit around waiting for the enemy to prey on our children. The world system will not suck them in; instead, we will fortify them and send them as change agents into the same system to influence their generation and the ones after them.

We are embarking on a 30 days prayer challenge on behalf of our children according to the scriptures in Mark 9:23, "All things are possible to him that believes".

Genesis 11:6, NIV: "The LORD said if as one people speaking the same language they have begun to do this, then nothing they plan to do will be impossible for them".

I believe that the next 30 days will go down in history for our children, as we would raise our voices to heaven, where ever we may be, home, work, school, traffic, anywhere, we would pray in our understanding and the spirit, we would push, and something is bound to happen when moms pray.

The mode of operation can be an individual mother or a group of mothers using this manual to rekindle their prayer altar for their children or for warfare or to fill their children's prayer bank, it could be used one month, a year or repeated monthly.

Tools needed for Moms prayer challenge as used by Jochebed.

Who is Jochebed?

Jochebed was a daughter of Levi (Exodus 2:1), and she was also the mother of Aaron, Moses, and Miriam

(Exodus 6:20; Numbers 26:59). Jochebed was married to Amram. To protect Moses from Pharaoh's command that every male Hebrew child should be killed, she placed him in an ark of bulrushes on the river. After Pharaoh's daughter discovered the baby, Jochebed became his nurse. She is noted among the heroes of faith in Hebrews 11.

The first tool we would need for this prayer challenge is faith in Christ Jesus, if you are not a believer sustaining faith then you are not a believer of Christ. Faith takes its anchor from the word of God, so we would be praying scriptures.

The mother of Moses is famous in the eyes of God not because she bore the baby Moses, but because of her faith—a faith that knew no defeat; Faith is one of the most frequently used words in the Christian vocabulary, but it may be one of the most misunderstood words. We are looking at the aspect of "Faith" in this lesson, not as saving faith, but as sustaining faith. Every genuine believer in Christ has already demonstrated saving faith, but sustaining faith speaks of the simple trust in God that one needs to exercise daily, to live a victorious Christian life, and to serve God acceptably. Sustaining faith in simple language is the assurance that the thing which God has said in His Word is true, and that God will act according to what He has said. Surely the words of Hebrews 11:6, "Without faith, it is impossible to please God" include the concept of sustaining faith.

The second tool we need is a gentle spirit also _known as calmness, not a fearful spirit. 1 Peter 3:4 (New American Standard 1977) let it be the hidden person_ of the heart, with the imperishable quality of a gentle and quiet spirit, which is precious in the sight of God.

We are building a prayer bank for 30 days that would last our children for the next 30 years, so we cannot rush it, we must carefully bank them with understanding and not fear, knowing that when our children get to the point where they need to withdraw from this bank, it would yield for them.

Jochebed was expecting a new arrival in her family, and she was aware of the consequence of having a male child—the decree was that the male babies would have to perish in the Nile River—and if the parents disobeyed, they too were subject to death.

Surely this was a time of great trial for Jochebed, but instead of manifesting fear and despair, she seemed to have confidence and hope. When the child was born, the baby was a boy, and we learn in Exodus 2:10 that he was later named "Moses." The God of Israel was more real to Amram and Jochebed than the king of Egypt. We learn that secret by reading Hebrews 11:23, which says, "By faith Moses, when he was born, was hid three months by his parents, because they saw that he was a proper child, and they were not afraid of the king's commandment, " Moses was hidden in his home for three months, and then in the reeds by the river, not because Jochebed could not bear to see her child perish, or because she loved him too much to cast him into the river. It was "by faith" that he was hidden, not by fear!

The parents of Moses believed the simple promise of God's Word and the revelation that after 400 years Israel would be delivered, and that their son was a "proper" child—and so, instead of casting baby Moses into the river, they hid him for three months and then turned him over to God.

The third tool is trustworthiness and action.

We must trust in the power and ability of God to help us take the appropriate steps more than the graveness of the current situation.

Jochebed had such a deep abiding faith and trust in God's Word that it drove her to act. She did not sit down and brood about the current situation in Egypt, and say, "If this child is to be Israel's deliverer, God will somehow spare him and deliver him; there's nothing we can do; so we'll throw him in the river, and if God wants him, He should save him."

She knew that God expects us to do our part and that He will not do for us what we can do for ourselves. God could grow a crop of wheat on the concrete pavements of our cities if He wanted to, but He expects the farmer to use the means at his disposal to grow a crop of wheat.

Jochebed did not say, "I'm going to throw the child into the river; if he's God's man, God will somehow save him." That is not faith; that is fanaticism. Faith is not testing God by jumping off bridges or having oneself deliberately bitten by rattlesnakes. And so

Jochebed did what she could. She hid Moses for some time, but as the child's lungs developed it became impossible to hide him. And when she could no longer hide him, she made a little basket, sealed it with pitch, and put the child in the basket, and laid it among the reeds by the river's brink (Exodus 2:3). And after Jochebed did all that she could, she went back home—undoubtedly with a great sense of trust that God would work things out according to His plan. Jochebed complied with the royal decree, but in protecting the child from the deep waters of the river, the essential point of the decree (killing the male babies) was disregarded.

All of these activities carried out by Jochebed are synonymous with prayers, just as we are about to pray and take actions on behalf of our children as inspired by God.

The fourth tool is to be expectant of God's intervention.

We need to know and believe that God has heard our prayers and He would begin to move things in the favor of our children, see the result that we want, keep it before us and expect it.

Beginning In verse 4, the book of Exodus 2, we see how God, in response to the faith of this mother who dared to trust in His word, He sets in motion a whole chain of wonderful events to accomplish His purposes and to honor her faith.

First of all, God began to move upon the heart of the daughter of a pagan king, so that at the exact time the baby Moses lay by the river's edge, Pharaoh's daughter came to this very place to take a swim. One wonders why Pharaoh's daughter wanted to take a bathe herself in the dirty waters of the Nile river. We know from history that all the kings in Pharaoh's day had bathhouses, such as even the wealthiest do not possess in our day. But Exodus 2:5 says that the daughter of Pharaoh came down to bathe in the river, while her attendants walked beside the river.

There was something supernatural and marvelous taking place here. This was God responding to the faith of a mother who dared to trust in Him. And when the little crib was brought to Pharaoh's daughter, she saw that it was a little Hebrew baby. We must remember that the young woman was the king's daughter and that the hatred for the Israelites was bred into the very core of her being. The expected thing for her to do was to have the little boy tilted over into the water. But we see God behind the scenes! The Scripture says, "And, behold, the babe wept" (Exodus 2:6). God saw to it that the baby should weep at this very moment. (Maybe an angel stood there and pinched the baby so that he would cry at the right time.)

The fifth tool is to be alert and available for your reward.

When God moves, He does it in mysterious ways, and we need to be proactive to know what to do when God begins to reward our acts of faith, it would be too good to be true, and we must seize the opportunity.

Genuine faith also has rewards. Not only was Moses spared, but his older sister (later identified as Miriam in Exodus 15:20), who was standing somewhere within sight; offered the Egyptian princess her services, and the princess told the little slave girl to go and get a nurse of the Hebrew women, and when she came back with their mother, Pharaoh's daughter said to her, "Take this child away and nurse it for me, and I will give thee thy wages. And the woman took the child, and nursed it" (Exodus 2:9).

A careful reader of the Bible account can almost picture Miriam (the older sister of Moses) running to her mother and telling her what had happened. I think we can imagine the fond expression on the mother's face as she says with great joy, "I knew that God would provide!" Jochebed's faith was rewarded by being reunited with her child. In fact, the goodness and mercy of God were so great that she was paid for nursing her son! God's providence was seeing to it that Jochebed was being paid from royal funds to look after her child. This is a clear example of how God gives, provides, and answers more abundantly than we can ever ask or think (Ephesians 3:20). That's how God does things. He does them in a big way if we dare to trust Him.

Dear Mums, with these tools, we are going to be standing in the gap for the survival and enthronement into the purpose of our children, they shall fulfill God's mandate for their lives, no harm or evil shall befall them, they shall be agents of change in their society.

(Research Materials on Jochebed are culled from Bible Helps Inc, Harold .S. Martins).

The sacrifices of a Mother from the eyes of Jochebed.

The meaning of Jochebed is "Jehovah is her or our Glory". She represents every mother who would rise to protect their children. Jehovah indeed is our glory.

Jochebed had three children, and each of them became well-known in their circle of influence. (Numbers 26). They were deeply rooted in faith because of their godly mother.

Moses became one of the greatest leaders and lawmakers the world has ever known, Aaron became Israel's first high priest and the founder of the Aaronic priesthood and Miriam, was a gifted prophetess, poetess, and musician. The three leaders were knitted as a family, their bond was unbreakable.

Jochebed gained a prominent place in the divine gallery, she gained the right and worthiness to be mentioned in the hall of faith, and to be placed among the heroines of faith in Hebrews 11. As mentioned in the scripture, her cleverly thought-out design to preserve the life of her baby boy, her courage and trust in such an act had such great effect on the nation, and the world at large. (Exodus 1, 2 and 6)

What exactly did Jochebed do to earn her this meritorious mention amongst the "great cloud of witnesses" whose lives and labour showcased their faith in God's faithfulness?

Pharaoh gave the dastardly order to kill all male born children of the Hebrew slaves, and Jochebed happened to be pregnant at that time. I can imagine that she was very apprehensive and uncertain about the future of her unborn child, if he were a boy.

The moment she saw her baby, she made up her mind to fight to save him. It was recorded three times in the Bible that "she saw that he was a goodly child" (Exodus 11, Acts 2, Hebrew 11)

This means that Moses was not just a lovely baby to look at, but also, he was a child with a great purpose. He was a 'change agent', implying that there was something greater than his looks and Jochebed owned the vision of God for Moses. She may not have been able to place her hands on her gut feeling, but she knew she had to do all it takes to preserve him.

The truth is that every child is a type of 'Moses', 'goodly and purposeful' once you can look deep enough with the heart and eyes of Jochebed.

How she managed to keep him quiet throughout the search of Pharaoh's soldiers was a mystery. Jochebed must have believed that since Moses was sent by God, only Him would be able to save Moses. We must as mothers get to that point where we hand our children over to God, knowing fully well in our hearts that they came from Him and He will preserve them. I have seen God move in this line many times in my journey with Him. Just like Jochebed, our faith in God, no matter how little coupled with our love for our children will propel us to make the necessary sacrifices and take the right steps for their safety and fulfilment of their purpose.

When Jochebed could no longer conceal Moses from the glaring eyes of the Egyptian soldiers. "God through the strength of her faith made her to see a vision of what He had planned for Moses," She made a little cradle of reeds which were believed to be protection against crocodiles, then placed the cradle with her son secretly among the bushes at the river's bank and told Miriam her young daughter to stand near to watch over the cradle made by her own hands. This implies that we are to help our children build the craft that will navigate them to their place of development and purpose. The brief but explicit account of what happened was given by Moses himself who, in his later years, by divine inspiration wrote the first five books of the Bible.

Jochebed must have sacrificed her time to learn how and what materials to use in building the floating craft. She dedicated her time to finishing the crafted basket that would house her baby to safety. The basket had to be able to support the baby, navigate smoothly on water, keep water out and keep the crocodiles at bay, as well as serve as an attraction to the daughter of Pharaoh. She must have also worked at night so that no one would see her. There must have been other moms who had male babies just like her, which was pushing her to take a stance when others gave up on the hope of saving their babies.

Jochebed put a lot of thoughts and work into making the floating. basket. Just like Jochebed, nothing is too much to dare, and our fervent prayers for our children would keep them supported and push them towards their destiny, it would prevent them from drowning in all that is happening in the society, it would keep the enemies at bay, and it would attract favor from their helpers of destiny.

Jochebed lived for God, and her sons and daughter were ignited by her fire for the Lord. She influenced her children to greatness. Although her children were not perfect as the story unfolded in the bible, but they performed great acts for God and served the people of God, hence fulfilling their purpose in life. Wow! A mother who caught the revelation of the purpose of God for her children, raised them according to the template of heaven, through divine guidance to deliver a whole nation from bondage and lead them through their wilderness experience on their way to the promised land.

Jochebed may not have lived to see the manifestation of the full result of her sacrifice, but I believe she was a fulfilled and happy mother, knowing that she did her possible best for her children. It was Jochebed's love, faith, and courage that saved her child from a brutal death and made it possible for him to be a blessing to the world.

Great things happen when moms pray, the destinies of our children are being molded as we do so. God help us all as we enjoy our Moment.

Atinuke Kuti
Jochebed's Mothers Circle

Instructions about the prayer challenge.

These are simple but effective scripture-based prayers.

It would require us individually lifting our voices in our understanding and the spirit between 11 pm - 12 am every day for the next one month.

Read up the scripture-based prayer points every morning, you should meditate and confess it into the lives of your children all through the day but at 11 pm you or together with your women group should gather on your online platform to pray.

This prayer challenge is meant to encourage and build each mom up in the place of regular prayers and confession for our children. It would be tasking but the sacrifice will be worth your while, as you will experience results and your children's prayer bank would be full.

During the day, be alert in your spirit and write

down instructions that will be given to you by the Holy Spirit.

Have faith and believe that your prayers are effective and it would make tremendous power available.

If you would like to encourage other moms all over the world to participate in filling their children's prayer bank, take a picture of yourself using this prayer guide and post on social media with #momspray.

May we and our children experience the revival and transformation that comes from collective prayers. Amen!

Day

Insert the names of your children

Psalm 127:3-5 ISV

Children are a gift from the LORD; a productive womb, the LORD's reward. As arrows in the hand of a warrior, so also are children born during one's youth. How blessed is the man whose quiver is full of them! He will not be ashamed as they confront their enemies at the city gate.

We start with thanking God for the calling of Motherhood, we thank Him for the gifts of His heritage, for the arrows in our hands that will help us confront the enemies at the gate. We will be thanking God that we will not be ashamed in Jesus Name.

We need to acknowledge that our children are not ours, but Gods. We need to thank Him for them because they are a gift given to us on lease. Just like Hannah did, we hand them over to God for use in His house, and just like Jochebed, we hand them over to God for use in the palaces and societies of this world to bring about transformation.

Arrows are weapons of warfare, and a warrior does not joke with his arrows. He sharpens and protects them, then he shoots them at the enemy, but if not protected they can be dangerous in the hands of the enemy. If not well sharpened they will not hit the target.

Prayers

We pray that God will give us the grace to sharpen them early with the word of God, good training, and values. When they are older, we pray that they will target and hit the enemy, and they will not be tools in the hands of the enemy against us. They will confront life's challenges because they are sharp arrows, and they will not put us to shame in Jesus Name. Amen!

**Lord, we thank You for You have heard and answered us in Jesus Name. Amen!*

Meditation/Action Plan

1.____

____

____

____

2.____

____

____

____

3.____

____

____

____

4.____

____

____

____

5.____

____

____

____

Day

Insert the names of your children and pray

Psalm 91:1-9 (Easy English Version)

Whoever stays in the secret place of the Most High will remain under the shadow of the Almighty. *I will say to the LORD, "(You are) my safe place and my strong castle. (You are) my God and I am trusting in You".* **He (God) really will save you from the trap that the bird-catcher (hid). And He (God) will save you from illnesses that cause death. He will cover you with His feathers. You will be safe under His wings. He (God) will do what He promised. And He will be like a big and small shields over you. Do not be afraid of:**

*   Bad spirits at night,
*   or the arrow that flies in the day,
*   or illnesses that come when it is dark,
*   or something bad that may destroy you at midday.

A thousand (people) may die by your side, ten thousand (people) may die by your right hand. But (the danger) will not come near to you. Your eyes will see it and watch, while it destroys bad

people. *For you, LORD, make me safe.* The Most High is your home, bad things will not happen to you. And there will be no fighting near where you live.

Prayers

Because our children dwell in the secret place of the most high, they abide under the shadow of the Almighty, we lift them up in the face of different viruses or diseases flying around like arrows, they shall not come near them in Jesus Name. They are fortified by the blood of Jesus. Amen!

Sometimes a child that has been displaying a high level of seriousness in academics and other areas of life suddenly becomes carefree. We pray that every virus/ arrow/spirit of flippancy will not find its root or way near our children in Jesus Name. Amen!

We address all illnesses that cause death as covered in verses 3 and 6 of Psalm 91. We say our children are shielded and protected in Jesus Name. We bring them under the covering of the blood of Jesus. Amen!

Our children will find God as their safe place (verse 2), the place of refuge. In times of trouble, they will not turn to drugs, immorality, nor alcohol, neither will they turn to bad influence. Their first and only option will be God in Jesus Name. Amen!

There is so much to fear in this dispensation, and the torment of fear is not about to get any less; however, our children shall not be afraid in Jesus Name, as verses 4-8 has given them the antidote to fear. Our children will not be fearful, and fear will not paralyze their destinies in Jesus Name. Amen!

It takes bravery to see thousands of people dying around you and not panic or be afraid, but verse 7 - 8 says it all. We pray for bravery for our children, and they will not be moved by the evil they see around them because, in the Name of Jesus, it will not come near them. Amen!

We pray that God will give His angels charge over them, to protect them everywhere they go in life, and they will not fall into the trap of the devil, particularly enemies pretending to be friends in Jesus Name. Amen!

We pray that our children will set their love on God so that He will honor them; when they call He will answer and deliver them from evil.

Our children will not die in our lifetime, God will satisfy them with long life, and they will experience His salvation in Jesus Name. Amen!

*Lord, we thank You for You have heard and answered us in Jesus Name. Amen!

Meditation/Action Plan

1.____

____

____

____

2.____

____

____

____

3.____

____

____

____

4.____

____

____

____

5.____

____

____

____

Day

Insert the names of your children and pray

Number 6:24-26 (Easy English Version)

**24 They must say, "I pray that the *LORD will *bless you. I pray that the*LORD will keep you safe.
25 I pray that the *LORD will smile at you. And I pray that he will be very kind to you.
 26 I pray that the *LORD will look at you. And I pray that He will give*peace to you."**

Prayers

This prayer covers every aspect of our children's lives. It is known as the priestly prayer; it is a confession of who they are becoming, a royal priesthood.

We pray that the blessings of God will manifest in their lives in Jesus Name. Amen!

The Lord's protection will be upon their lives during this academic Session.

The favor of God will envelop them all around, and He will show them his kindness in all they do and in everywhere they go in Jesus Name. Amen!

The Lord will cause His glory to radiate around them and give them peace of mind in Jesus Name. Amen!

Safety is of the Lord, the Bible in Psalm 127:1 says except the Lord builds the house, those who build are laboring in vain. We pray that God will continually keep our children safe in Jesus Name. Amen!

There is a difference between looking at someone and smiling at someone according to verses 25 and 26. To look at a person is to stare with the intent to understand the person; while smiling makes a facial gesture that assures the person that I am with you. God will look at our children so He can smile on them, and their hearts will be filled with joy as the Lord smiles on them in Jesus Name. Amen!

When God looks at you, he sees the hidden things that man cannot see; we pray that God will reveal our children to us in Jesus Name. The things that we need to know about them, to help them navigate through life or correct them in love, will be revealed to us by God and He will show us the hidden things in the Name of Jesus. (Jeremiah 33:3) Amen!

**Lord, we thank You for You have heard and answered us in Jesus Name. Amen!*

Meditation/Action Plan

1. ____

____

____

____

2. ____

____

____

____

3. ____

____

____

____

4. ____

____

____

____

5. ____

____

____

____

Day

Insert the names of your children and pray

Ephesians 1:18 (BBE version)
And that having the eyes of your heart full of light, you may have knowledge of what is the hope of His purpose, what is the wealth of the glory of His heritage in the saints.

At some point in the life of Moses, he understood that he was not meant to be enthroned in Egypt; though he had lived as a prince in Egypt. Israel was his destination, and He had to embrace His purpose. We pray our children will come to an understanding of their purpose in life, and they will not make their Egypt the place of enthronement, despite the level of comfort they might have attained there in Jesus Name. Amen!

Prayers

The eyes of our children will be full of light, that their identity will not be hidden from them in Jesus Name. Amen!

Our children will not grope in the darkness of trying to fit in when they have a custom-made assignment / place in destiny. It shall be made known to them early in life in Jesus Name. Amen!

It is one thing to understand your purpose and another thing to have the willpower to push through. Our children will have the inner strength and physical strength to push through their purpose in Jesus Name. Amen!

The peer pressure at every level, will not derail our children from their purpose in Jesus Name. Amen!

When the purpose of a thing or someone is not discovered, abuse is inevitable. Our children will not abuse their lives and future family in Jesus Name. Amen!

When the purpose of a thing or someone is not discovered, others will use you to achieve their purpose. Our children will collaborate with others to help them fulfill a purpose, but they will not be used to fulfill other people's purposes without discovering theirs, in Jesus Name. Amen!

When their purpose is discovered, life is easier and full of Joy. Our children will have their journeys easier and full of joy in Jesus Name. Amen!

**Lord, we thank You for You have heard and answered us in Jesus Name. Amen!*

Meditation/Action Plan

1.____

____

____

____

2.____

____

____

____

3.____

____

____

____

4.____

____

____

____

5.____

____

____

____

Day

5

Insert the names of your children and pray

Isaiah 11:2 - 3 (Easy English Version)
The Spirit of the *LORD will come on him. It will be:
* a *Spirit that knows what is right; and one that knows what things mean
* a *Spirit that tells people the right thing to do and one that has authority
* a *Spirit that knows everything and one that is afraid to make the*LORD angry.

3 To obey the *LORD will give pleasure to the Branch. He will not decide about things (only) with what his eyes see. He will not decide (only) with what his ears hear.

Prayers

Our children will possess the seven spirits of God and operate in the fear of the Lord, which is the beginning of application of knowledge in Jesus Name. Amen!

Pray that these seven spirits / abilities would rest upon your children.

The spirit of the Lord is the spirit that helps them to find their way to the Lord, our children would never be lost. They would always find their way to the right path in Jesus Name. Amen!

The spirit of counsel and might is the ability to take instructions, take action, and excel excellently. They will always have the ability and the drive to take steps and accomplish every set task. Someone can have the ability but no drive or vice versa, but our children would have both in Jesus Name. Amen!

The spirit of wisdom and understanding is the ability to apply knowledge, and gain insight into everything; as our children go through life, they will know what to do, how to do it, and understand the puzzles of life in Jesus Name. Amen!

The spirit of knowledge and the fear of the Lord is the ability to gather accurate information and know the ones to believe and discard because of the obedience they would have towards the Lord. We would not be afraid of our children getting certain information because we know they have the fear of the Lord; they choose the right information to act on in Jesus Name. Amen!

The spirit of creativity is the ability to imagine and create; a creative person can never be stranded. Our children would always find a way to solve any problem that comes their way (In academic or life), they will never be stranded in Jesus Name. Amen!

Our children will be sensitive to God and His promptings in Jesus Name, and when they need to make a life decision, they will hear God and follow through in Jesus Name. Amen!

Our children will not judge any situation, circumstance or persons based on surface value, but they will be in tune with the Holy Spirit always, and their pleasure will be to obey God in Jesus Name. Amen!

The fear of the Lord is a spirit (verse 2b). Once they possess it, it would guide their every action, and you won't need to scold them; they will be mindful of their steps because they fear God. We pray that our children will have the spirit of the fear of God in Jesus Name. Amen!

**Lord, we thank You, for You have heard and answered us in Jesus Name. Amen!*

Meditation/Action Plan

1. ____
____
____
____

2. ____
____
____
____

3. ____
____
____
____

4. ____
____
____
____

5. ____
____
____
____

Day

Insert the names of your children and pray

Exodus 35:31, 35 (Easy English Version)
The Lord has filled him with the Spirit of God and has made him very wise. He knows how to make many different things.

The *Lord has given them very *wise minds that are full of good ideas. They draw plans of beautiful things, and then they make them. They use many different materials to make lovely things. And they are both masters at their work.'

1 Corinthians 2:16 BBE
For who has knowledge of the mind of the Lord, so as to be his teacher? But we have the mind of Christ.

Prayers

We pray that our children have the mind of God, so they are creative, they are solution providers, and in their mind and hands lies the answers to the world's problems.

1. God has wonderful things prepared to tell and give to all those who have truly come to know Him. God will reveal to our children those things which human understanding alone will never see like scientific inventions, cures to diseases, discoveries in the universe, creative solutions to transportation, climate change, housing, education, entertainment, and so on in Jesus Name. *Amen!*

2. These things are understood through spiritual illumination. God will give our children spiritual insight into things, and they will become experts in their work in Jesus Name. *Amen!*

3. The one who knows a man best is his spirit, no one knows you better than you. In the same way, the one who knows God best is His Holy Spirit. He knows everything in the mind of God. Our children will be filled with the Holy Spirit so they can have access to the mind of God in Jesus Name. *Amen!*

4. We have received God's Spirit—if we are true followers of Christ, He is in us! Therefore, we have the mind of Christ in us and the capacity to know everything we need to know from God. Our children will be true followers of God so that they can operate in the

mind of God in Jesus Name. Amen!

5. The things we could not have understood before we received the Spirit; we can now understand through the Spirit's help. A man without the Spirit cannot understand these things; they are spiritually appraised (like a jeweler appraises a diamond and see the realities that a natural and untrained eye could never see). Our children's spirit will be Intune with God, that their mind will be trained to pick the signals of God, and they will have more understanding than their peers in Jesus Name. Amen!

6. These things are freely given to us by God. He is not trying to withhold them from us or playing games; If we cooperate with Him and listen, He will make them known by His Spirit and His Word. Our children will always cooperate with the Holy Spirit so they can have a dynamic mind in Jesus Name. Amen!

7. Once we learn these things from God's Spirit and His Word, we can share them with others through the power of spiritual words. Our children will develop the capacity to share the insight they have received from God with other people in Jesus Name. Amen!

As they share the insight they have received with others, their mind will not be corrupted in Jesus Name; and they will receive the wisdom to convert the knowledge into tangible solutions that will make them sought after in the mighty Name of Jesus. Amen!

**Lord, we thank You for You have heard and answered us in Jesus Name. Amen!*

Meditation/Action Plan

1.____
____
____
____

2.____
____
____
____

3.____
____
____
____

4.____
____
____

5.____
____
____

Day

Insert the names of your children and pray

Isaiah 54:13 ISV
Then all your children will be taught by the LORD, and great will be your children's prosperity.

Isaiah 54:14 (Easy English Version)
The *LORD will build you on a *base of what is right. You will be a long way from cruel people. Really, you will have nothing to be afraid of. Nobody will ever frighten you again. People who frighten you will not come near to you.

Prayers

God will not leave our children to themselves in Jesus Name, and they shall make themselves available to be taught of the Lord. Amen!

As they are taught, they shall enjoy prosperity in all spheres (Mind, body, Spirit, Academics, Career, relationships), in Jesus Name. Amen!

We shall enjoy peace of mind when our children are taught of the Lord, we receive peace of mind over our children in Jesus Name. Amen!

The Lord himself will build our children on the right foundation in Jesus Name. We uproot every wrong family foundation that can affect our children Negatively, and we shield them with the Blood of Jesus from walking in the errors of their parents in Jesus Name. Amen!

We cover our children with the Blood of Jesus and declare that they will be far away from their enemies in Jesus Name. Amen!

The enemy's plan will not prevail over them in the Name of Jesus. Our children will always hold their peace.

Our children will have no cause to fear anyone or anything, and no one and nothing shall frighten them in Jesus Name. Amen!

Evil hands and eyes will not have access to our children, and they will not come near them in Jesus Name. Amen!

In the Name of Jesus, the prosperity of our children shall be great and visible to all in Jesus Name. *Amen!*

**Lord, we thank You for You have heard and answered us in Jesus Name. Amen!*

Meditation/Action Plan

1.____

____

____

____

2.____

____

____

____

3.____

____

____

____

4.____

____

____

____

5.____

____

____

____

Day

Insert the names of your children and pray

Isaiah 8:18 (Easy English Version)
Here am I and the children that the LORD has given to me. We are messages. We are messages from the LORD who lives on the mountain called Zion.

Prayers

We pray that our children will reflect what we represent, and that they become the message of God's expression; they are the signs and wonders of God's mercies, goodness, and faithfulness so that they will represent God and us well in the society in Jesus Name. Amen!

Our children will be messages of love to a world deprived of true and pure love. True love gives without demanding. (For God so love the world that He Gave... (John 3:16)). He did not demand anything from us other than for us to receive His love; He gave to save. We live in a world where you give to get (This is not God's kind of love). We pray in Jesus Name that our Children will be the message of God's kind of love. Amen!

Our children will be messages of God's power and ability, and they will be able to do that which seems impossible to others in Jesus Name. Amen!

Our children will be messages of God's faithfulness, and even amid adverse circumstances, they shall experience the faithful intervention of God in Jesus Name. Amen!

Our children will be messages of God's resilience, if God can be resilient in the face of human abuse of His power and love, he did not destroy the world despite our offences. Our children will display God's resilience amid offences in Jesus Name. Amen!

Our children will be messages of God's fruitfulness in Jesus Name. They shall be fruitful in all they do and in every area of life. Amen!

Our children shall display God's creative power, they shall come up with mind-blowing innovations in Jesus Name. Amen!

Our children are messages of God's fearlessness in a fearful world. Our children will not manifest the spirit of fear and panic, we cast it out of them in Jesus Name, they will not take action based on fear, they shall be calm in the face of crisis in Jesus Name. Amen!

*Lord, we thank You for You have heard and answered us in Jesus Name. Amen!

Meditation/Action Plan

1. _______________________________________

____

____

____

2. _______________________________________

____

____

____

3. _______________________________________

____

____

____

4. _______________________________________

____

____

____

5. _______________________________________

____

____

____

Day

Insert the names of your children and pray

Deuteronomy 28:13 (BBE Version)
The Lord will make you the head and not the tail; and you will ever have the highest place, if you give ear to the orders of the Lord your God which I give you today, to keep and to do them;

Prayers

We ask that God gives our children the hearing ears to obey and follow instructions that will make them leaders in their generation. Amen!

Our children shall always manifest leadership qualities that will position them in the highest quarters where ever they find themselves in Jesus Name. Amen!

Being the head means you are one step ahead of everyone else; our children will never fall behind in anything in Jesus Name. They will always be many steps above their contemporaries and their enemies in Jesus Name. Amen!

The tail is always dragged around and tossed to and fro. Our children will never be tossed around in life by their contemporaries or enemies in Jesus Name; they will be as firm as the head, coordinating their affairs with precision and the help of the Holy Spirit in the Name of Jesus. Amen!

The strategy that they need to maintain the head and not tail in their academics and other areas of life; God would give to them in Jesus Name. Amen!

Our children will be starting their examination week. Let us commit them into the hands of God, they shall be strong and healthy and maintain the head position. Their academic performance will not drop in Jesus Name. Amen!

The peace and calm of God shall reign in their heart, and they shall not be distracted by fear or its cohorts in Jesus Name. Amen!

Any child who is having academic challenges shall be helped by God to discover his or her learning style and strategy; they will adopt and be the head in Jesus Name. Amen!

God will bridge the gap between the learning abilities of our children and the demands of their Examination and they will become tops in Jesus Name. Amen!

We lift our voices to pray and confess on them today, that they shall remain the head and not the tail, they shall be above and not beneath in Jesus Name. Amen!

If you are pregnant, place your hands on your tummy and pray the same prayers.

**Lord, we thank You for You have heard and answered us in Jesus Name. Amen!*

Meditation/Action Plan

1.____

2.____

3.____

4.____

5.____

Day

Insert the names of your children and pray

Psalm 119:99 (BBE Version)
I have more knowledge than all my teachers because I give thought to Your unchanging word.

Prayers

We pray that our children will learn how to be self-motivated to study and meditate on the word of God and their academic work; so that they can have more insight than their Sunday school teachers and class teachers, as a result, they would be able to ask the right questions and excel. Amen!

The ability to have foresight is from the Lord. The ability to understand patterns through knowledge is of God; we pray that our children will be full of God's word and the ability to proffer solutions to the happenings around them and it will be evident to all in the Name of Jesus. Amen!

Concerning their academics, we pray that our children would learn to study ahead of the class and their teachers' scheme of work, such that when they are asked questions in the classroom, their answers will challenge the teachers or lecturers. Amen!

We pray that the desire to know more would be kindled in them, and they shall be of an excellent spirit in Jesus Name. Amen!

We cast out every spirit of forgetfulness in our children's life, rather they will inspire their classmates to want to be more knowledgeable and inspire their teachers to be on their toes.

This prayer also goes beyond the classroom; it addresses other areas of their lives where they are tutored.

They would have a good understanding of life and its requirements, and they will fulfil purpose in Jesus Name. Amen!

This sort of knowledge comes from studying and meditating on God's word. We pray that our children will turn to digest God's word regularly and meditate on it constantly, even more than they do with social media or their electronic games in Jesus Name. Amen!

As we lift our voices today on behalf of our children, we declare that our children learn to meditate on God's word so they can have a better understanding than their teachers and make discoveries. Sir Isaac Newton meditated so much on God's word and nature to discover the first law of motion and other laws he discovered, so shall it be in our children's life in Jesus Name. Amen!

Those who are more knowledgeable lead and others follow. Our children will always lead because they will be knowledgeable always in Jesus Name. Amen!

**Lord, we thank You for You have heard and answered us in Jesus Name. Amen!*

Meditation/Action Plan

1.____

____

____

____

2.____

____

____

____

3.____

____

____

____

4.____

____

____

____

5.____

____

____

____

Day

Insert the names of your children and pray

Isaiah 49:23 (WEB Version)
Kings shall be your foster fathers, and their queens your nursing mothers. They will bow down to you with their faces to the earth, and lick the dust of your feet. Then you will know that I am Yahweh, and those who wait for Me shall not be disappointed."

Prayers

We pray that our children will find favor with high-profile leaders, the best in the land of their dwelling. They would help to guide them and make provisions for them as if they were their children. Amen!

Our children will enjoy the type of favor that will make them sought after by kings/ leaders in the world; The sort of favor that will make leaders bow down to them and yield to their desires. Amen!

We pray that wherever our children go, they would get first-class treatment, be pampered, and preferred above all. Amen!

We pray that people in high places will find themselves taking care of our children because they will find favor in their sight. Amen!

We pray that our children will have access to the best mentors in life in Jesus Name. The wrong mentors can do more harm than good, so in the Name of Jesus, we call forth the best mentors for them in Jesus Name. Amen!

Our children will wine and dine with greatness, and their gift will make them stand before kings and not mean men. We pray for mentors with the mentality of kings and queens for our children in Jesus Name. Amen!

Our children will manifest the etiquettes and conduct that will take them and sustain them in the palace in Jesus Name. Amen!

Moses was found and raised by royalty, but Jochebed prepared him in the first 6years of life for his destiny, as mothers God will enable us to do the needful in raising our children for the palace (The high place for the fulfillment of destiny), in Jesus Name. Amen!

Our children will learn through their relationship with God that those that wait on Him will never be disappointed. God will never disappoint them in Jesus Name. *Amen!*

I declare today that kings and queens are the nursing parents of our children. *Amen!*

They (Our children) shall be mentored by the noble and the great in the land, they shall be favored by the movers and shakers of the land, institution, location or industry, where ever our children find themselves, this prayer would speak for them in Jesus Name. *Amen!*

Lord, we thank You for You have heard and answered us in Jesus Name. Amen!

Meditation/Action Plan

1.____

2.____

3.____

4.____

5.____

Day

12

Insert the names of your children and pray

Psalm 37:23 (NET Translation)
The LORD grants success to the one whose behaviour He finds commendable.

Prayers

We pray that our children will give attention to good training so that their behavior will be commendable, and the Lord will order their steps all through life to succeed in Jesus Name. Amen!

Their (our children) steps will be ordered into success and victory in Jesus Name. Amen!

We pray that our children will not step into irreversible trouble in Jesus Name. Amen!

Our children will not step into shame and error in Jesus Name. Amen!

They (our children) will not walk in the counsel of ungodly peers and will not stand in the way that sinners go in Jesus Name. Amen!

Our children will never step in, to sit with scorfers in Jesus Name. Amen!

Their steps will not be ordered into calamity in Jesus Name. Amen!

Their delight will be in the Lord, to do His will always.

Our children's steps will be navigated towards good spouses and families in Jesus Name. Amen!

They shall enjoy great success and victories in life in Jesus Name. Amen!

**Thank You, Lord, for answering us in Jesus Name. Amen!*

Meditation/Action Plan

1.____

____

____

____

2.____

____

____

____

3.____

____

____

____

4.____

____

____

____

5.____

____

____

____

Day

Insert the names of your children and pray

Proverbs 4:18 (Easy English Version)
But the road that good people travel along is like the sunrise. It gets brighter and brighter until it is really day.

Prayers

We pray that our children will grow up to be good people, and they will never grope in the dark; their path will shine until they get to their destination in Jesus Name. Amen!

Our children will never have a better yesterday in the Name of Jesus; there would be challenging situations, but the challenges would work together for their good and move them towards their destiny in the mighty Name of Jesus. Amen!

When our children come home with a result less than what they obtained the previous term, rather than judging them, we should encourage them, understand, and declare that their path is shining brighter and brighter unto a better day. Even when they fall, the light will shine on their way, so they can rise and continue on their journey in the Name of Jesus. Amen!

Our children's path will always be bright in Jesus Name, and we should encourage them to achieve and see possibilities and not allow anyone to fill them with negativity. A cloudy day does not indicate that the sun is not shining; once the cloud lifts, the day continues and still adds up to 24 hours. Time does not lose value because of a cloudy day; our children's sun will never wane. It will continue to shine, even on the darkest day in the mighty Name of Jesus. Amen!

As they (our children) journey through life, their path is enlightened, and they find destiny and everything good lined up for them on that path in Jesus Name. Amen!

Their path receives light to see the potholes and know how to avoid them; they will never fall into a hole they can evade in the Name of Jesus. Amen!

It is good to be mentored, but your mentor's path will not always be yours; you must be able to find your lane and navigate through with the gleanings obtained from your mentor. Our children will not walk in the path of others, and they will not walk in the tracks not meant for them. They will find their lane and navigate through it with our support in the Name of Jesus. Amen!

Our children will not walk blindfolded on their path, and they will not walk with the stubbornness of heart; they will listen to good counsel and see the light that brightens up their way in Jesus Name. Amen!

They (Our children) will develop the faith to trust their path as they journey along through the way; though it does not light up all at once, it will get brighter and brighter. Our children will never stop moving on their path, and they will always find the strength and motivation to keep moving and follow the brightness revealed as they journey in Jesus Name. Amen!

Lord, we thank You for You have heard and answered us in Jesus Name. Amen!

Meditation/Action Plan

1.____

____

____

____

2.____

____

____

____

3.____

____

____

____

4.____

____

____

____

5.____

____

____

____

Day

Insert the names of your children and pray

Act 5:34 -35 (Easy English Version)
But one man did not agree. He stood up in front of the Sanhedrin. He was called Gamaliel and he was a Pharisee, a teacher of the Law. All the men of the Sanhedrin liked Gamaliel. And they thought that he was a good man. Gamaliel asked the policemen to take the apostles out of the room.

When they had gone, Gamaliel spoke to the *Sanhedrin. 'Men of*Israel!' he said. 'Be careful about what you want to do. Think again before you kill these men.

One of the helpers of destiny in life is a person who defends you or your cause, where or when you can not protect yourself. Gamaliel vindicated the apostles from being killed. We pray that our children shall find a defender of their lives, goals, and causes as they navigate through life. God shall position a Gamaliel for them whenever the need arises in Jesus Name. Amen!

Prayers

Our children will never lack someone to defend them whenever they need one in Jesus Name. *Amen!*

Deceitful tongues will not trap our children; they will find people who will be willing to stand up for them in Jesus Name. *Amen!*

In the day of trouble, their Gamaliel shall rise to their defense in Jesus Name. *Amen!*

In their institutions, God will position a Gamaliel for them, who will defend their projects, their scores, their internship, their School activities, and so on in Jesus Name. *Amen!*

In their work God will raise a Gamaliel for them; someone to defend their proposals, their promotions, and applications in Jesus Name. *Amen!*

In their Marital life, God will position a Gamaliel for them if the need arises in Jesus Name. *Amen!*

The Gamaliel in our childrens' life will not have any

reason to be envious of them, and he or she will perform that which they have been assigned to do without seeking attention in Jesus Name. Amen!

Our children will never be in a situation where they cannot be bailed out by a Gamaliel, in Jesus Name. Amen!

*Lord, we thank You for You have heard and answered us in Jesus Name. Amen!

Meditation/Action Plan

1.____

____

____

____

2.____

____

____

____

3.____

____

____

____

4.____

____

____

____

5.____

____

____

____

Day

Insert the names of your children and pray

Numbers 10:28-31 (Easy English Version)
28 The Israelites marched out like that every time that they started to travel. 29 Moses spoke to Hobab. Hobab was the brother of Moses' wife. Hobab's father was Reuel who came from Midian. Moses said, 'We are leaving here now. We are going to another place. And the LORD has said, "I will give that place to you." The LORD has promised good things about Israel's people. So come with us and we will do good things for you.'

30 The Israelites marched out like that every time that they started to travel.

31 Then Moses said, 'But you know where we should camp in the desert. So please do not leave us. You can be like our eyes as we travel.

Our children need guardians when they need to navigate through unfamiliar terrain in life. We may not be there to guide them, but God knows the person (s) that will be ideal to lead them. Hobab helped Moses and the children of Israel to locate their way in the wilderness.

We pray that God will send a pathfinder/ navigator to our children, and they will not have to wander around before they get directions in life in Jesus Name. Amen!

Prayers

We pray that wherever our children are, any time they feel lost and need direction in life, God will send a Hobab to help them navigate their way in Jesus Name. Amen!

 God will always send someone to give them godly counsel and guidance in Jesus Name. Amen!

A Hobab can be anybody, either younger, older, or age mate, God will raise someone or people at any area of their life that would point them in the right direction in Jesus Name. Amen!

This prayer cuts across different age groups from 6 years and above, there are times when children need direction or guidance, and the wrong peers or people may be around them. As we step up as mothers to continue to lift them up in prayers, God would position the right people around them in the Name of Jesus. Amen!

I always tell my children that they should not succumb to the wrong peer pressure, but they should be good peer pressure. We pray that God will use our children as good peer pressure to influence their peers in the right direction in Jesus Name. Amen!

If the children of Israel were led into the camp of the enemy by their Hobab, they would not have seen it coming. Our children will not be deceived, in Jesus Name. Amen!

It is one thing for God to send a Hobab, but it is another for us to recognize and follow the Hobab. Our children will identify and be lead by their Hobab in Jesus Name. Amen!

God will direct a Hobab towards our children's path that would help them avoid unnecessary pit holes in their journey in Jesus Name. They will never lack the right direction in Jesus Name. Amen!

*Lord, we thank you for you have heard and answered us in Jesus Name. Amen!

Meditation/Action Plan

1.____

____

____

____

2.____

____

____

____

3.____

____

____

____

4.____

____

____

____

5.____

____

____

____

Day

16

Insert the names of your children and pray

Psalm 23:1 (Easy English Version)
The LORD is my shepherd. I will not need anything.

Prayers

Though the Lord is their shepherd, we pray that He would shepherd our children through the right mentors and leaders. He will send the good shepherds to them, and they will not live through life without being accountable to someone or cared for in Jesus Name. Amen!

The Lord will shepherd our children as they journey through life because the Lord is their shepherd, and they shall not lack for anything in Jesus Name. Amen!

It is one thing to shepherd someone but another for the shepherd to be accepted. Our children will accept the Lord as their shepherd for life in Jesus Name. Amen!

The Lord was the shepherd of Israel during their transit in the wilderness, but He also chose a physical shepherd, Moses. We ask that God will direct their part to a physical shepherd, after the heart of God and for the good of our children, in Jesus Name. *Amen!*

The old prophet in 1kings misled the young prophet. The shepherds in our children's lives will not mislead them in Jesus Name. *Amen!*

At different points in the journey of life, God may bring about a change of shepherd, and often if not handled with maturity, their destinies can be messed up. Our children will not encounter immature Shepherds that would not understand how and when to let them go fulfill purpose in Jesus Name. *Amen!*

Shepherds are helpers of destiny, but some shepherds end up destroying the future of their flock; our children will not be trampled on or delayed by their shepherds in Jesus Name. *Amen!*

Our children will recognize their shepherds when they see them; they will identify them by their fruits in Jesus Name. *Amen!*

*Lord, we thank You for You have heard and answered us in Jesus Name. *Amen!*

Meditation/Action Plan

1.______________________________

____

____

____

2.______________________________

____

____

____

3.______________________________

____

____

____

4.______________________________

____

____

____

5.______________________________

____

____

____

Day

17

Insert the names of your children and pray

Ezra 1:1-2 (Easy English Version)

1 Cyrus, king of Persia had just begun to rule Babylon. He decided to make a new law. Men wrote it down. And he sent out men with the news. He sent them to all the people that he ruled. God had caused him to do this. God had said to Jeremiah years before that He would send the Israelites home . 2 This is what Cyrus, the king of Persia said: 'The Lord, the God of heaven, has given me power over all the kingdoms on the earth. He has said that I must build a temple for Him in Jerusalem. That is the biggest city in Judah.

Cyrus supplied all that was needed to build the temple, even though he was not a Jew, but God instructed him to do it. Our children might have needs that we may not be able to meet, but as they learn to walk with God, we pray that He will raise people like Cyrus in their lives to supply their needs as He deems fit.

Prayers

Our children will never be financially stranded in life because the Lord will order the steps of their Cyrus to their way in Jesus Name. Amen!

Cyrus is not somebody you ask for money, but a Cyrus is a person whose conviction and direction is by God to meet your specific needs. Our children's Cyrus will be activated to help them on their journey in life, in Jesus Name. Amen!

The heart of our children's Cyrus will never be turned against them by mischief-makers, and our children's Cyrus will remember them at the appointed time in Jesus Name. Amen!

When our children have projects to develop, God will position their Cyrus to buy-in and support them in Jesus Name. Amen!

Our children will not dismiss their Cyrus by being rude or unruly, but they shall recognize their Cyrus in Jesus Name.Amen!.

A Cyrus can come in any way and much more to help our children fulfil their destinies.

Cyrus can be a person, system, or institution.
Cyrus as Person.
A Person: God can send someone who would regularly send money to help with the upkeep of the child or children, and it may come in as a favor or a loan, a timely job from an individual, that would yield financial gains. Cyrus can come indirectly into the hands of the older children in universities. We pray for the activation of this for any child who needs it in Jesus Name. *Amen!*

Cyrus as a system.

A System: An entitlement can come in for them from the state or federal government, or an inheritance from their grandparents, family members that love them could suddenly be bestowed on them. Part of the resources Cyrus gave to the Israelites for rebuilding the temple were items stolen from them by Nebuchadnezzar. Our children will not miss out on their entitlement, and whatever belongs to them will be restored to them by their Cyrus in Jesus Name. *Amen!*

Cyrus as an Institution

An Institution: They can be nominated for different types of scholarships by their schools. Like for various competitions. They can receive financial awards, financial aids, and bursaries. A company can engage them for internships and reward them greatly. Our children will be recognized and recommended by their Cyrus for provision in Jesus Name. Amen!

**Lord, we thank You for You have heard and answered us in Jesus Name. Amen!*

Meditation/Action Plan

1.____

____

____

____

2.____

____

____

____

3.____

____

____

____

4.____

____

____

____

5.____

____

____

____

Day

18

Insert your children's names

Genesis 20:14-16 (ISV Version) 14
So Abimelech took some sheep and oxen, and some male and female servants, gave them to Abraham, returned his wife Sarah to him, 15 and said, "Look! My land is available to you, so settle wherever you please." 16 Abimelech also told Sarah, "Look! I am giving your brother 1,000 pieces of silver to vindicate you in the eyes of all who are with you. As a result, you will be completely vindicated."

Abimelech, in this context, is someone who would help make room for our children in a foreign land, make them comfortable in a foreign land or place like they were residents. God will raise someone who will give them leverage in life in Jesus Name. Amen!

Abimelech can be anywhere for our children, from their School environment to their work station, home environment, and worship centers. God will reveal our children's Abimelech to them.

Prayers

We pray that anywhere our children find themselves in life, that God will raise someone who would make room for them in Jesus Name. Amen!

The person who would help them settle down in school by making the environment comfortable for them, when they travel to a foreign land, the person that would assist them in getting a soft landing, and leverage to succeed will come their way.

Oh! Lord, as Abimelech supplied all the flocks that Abraham needed to succeed in the animal rearing business, please send help to our children to give them the leverage they need in any new environment they find themselves in life in Jesus Name. Amen!

Abimelech gave free lands to Abraham to settle down with his family, giving him room and advantage in the terrain.

Oh, Lord! Send someone to make room for our children with ease, wherever they go in Jesus Name. Amen!

Abraham almost lost Abimelech by not being honest with him; our children will not engage in activities that discourage their Abimelech in Jesus Name. *Amen!*

Abimelech was in a position to take advantage of Abraham, but he did not. Our children's Abimelech will not take advantage of them in Jesus Name. *Amen!*

Abimelech made room for Abraham to prosper, and he became more prosperous than Abimelech, such that Abimelech became insecure (Gen 21:22). Our children's Abimelech will not be intimidated by our children's prosperity in Jesus Name. *Amen!*

Abimelech helped Abraham and Isaac to create generational wealth. Our children's Abimelech will help them create generational wealth in Jesus Name. *Amen!*

Abimelech will make all his machinery available for our children in Jesus Name. *Amen!*

Lord, we thank You for You have heard and answered us in Jesus Name. Amen!

Meditation/Action Plan

1._______________________________________

____

____

____

2._______________________________________

____

____

____

3._______________________________________

____

____

____

4._______________________________________

____

____

____

5._______________________________________

____

____

____

Day

19

Insert your children's names

Mark 15:21 (ISV Version)
They forced a certain passer-by named Simon of Cyrene, the father of Alexander and Rufus, who happened to be coming in from the country, to carry Jesus' cross.

Prayers

God shall send to you a Simon of Cyrene, and you shall never bear your burdens alone in Jesus Name. Amen!

This prayer helps to address the mental health of our children. Our children will not breakdown mentally in Jesus Name. Amen!

At different times in life, we might bear certain overwhelming burdens, and if there is no one to share them with or no one to give us the right support, it can become detrimental to their health. Our children will always get mental health support in Jesus Name. Amen!

When Jesus was carrying His heavy cross to Calvary, a man, Simon of Cyrene, was compelled to help Jesus bear the cross. He had no choice but to comply, So he helped Jesus bear His burden. Our children will always have a burden bearer as they journey in life in Jesus Name. *Amen!*

God will compel people to help our children lessen their burden on the Journey of life in Jesus Name. *Amen!*

Where ever our children find themselves, and in whatever circumstances they face, God shall raise for them a Simon of Cyrene, and they will never have to bear their burdens alone in Jesus Name. *Amen!*

Our children will never walk this life alone without a genuine burden bearer, who will not be a deceitful tale bearer but a helper of destiny in Jesus Name. *Amen!*

W.H.O predicts that depression will be the number one killer by 2030, in this generation of many online friends and few real-life friends; Our children will never be part of that statistic in Jesus Name. *Amen!*

Our children will receive the courage not to bottle in their emotions but would be able to open up to their burden bearers when the need arises in Jesus Name. *Amen!*

God will help people comply with the right directives to slow down and eradicate the spread of coronavirus, especially the young, restless, old and bored people in Jesus Name. Amen!

**Lord, we thank You for You have heard and answered us in Jesus Name. Amen!*

Meditation/Action Plan

1.____

2.____

3.____

4.____

5.____

Day

Insert your children's names

Genesis 49:22 (KJV)
Joseph *is* a fruitful bough, *even* a fruitful bough by a well; *whose* branches run over the wall:

Verses 23- 25 23 Even though enemies attacked him, shooting at him and pursuing him viciously, 24 nevertheless his bow remained steady and his arms kept in shape by the strength of Jacob's Mighty One, in the name of the Shepherd, Israel's Rock, 25 by your father's God who helps you, by the Almighty who will keep on blessing you with blessings from heaven above, with blessings from the deepest ocean, with the blessing from the breasts and the womb.

Prayers

This prayer is the best prayer you could ever pray for your child.

A fruitful bough means your children would always be prosperous in whatever they do because they are positioned by the well. They will never lack water, and they will always be productive even in the dry season in Jesus Name. *Amen!*

Their branches run over the wall meaning - no obstacle can stand before our children, and their branches will breakthrough every obstacle before them in Jesus Name. *Amen!*

No matter the issues that may arise in their lives, they will always find a way around or through it. They are unstoppable in Jesus Name.

Problems of life will never define them nor stop them from achieving their goals, and they will never give up in Jesus Name. *Amen!*

Our children will never be in a fix or mold that they cannot break out from in Jesus Name. *Amen!*

We commit our children into the hands of God, and we declare today that they are fruitful and productive; they will run over every obstacle or challenge that comes their way in Jesus Name. *Amen!*

Our children's enemies will never defeat them because our God will help them in Jesus Name. Amen!

The more the enemy comes at them, the stronger their defense will be because of the strength of Jacob's Mighty One, and the Rock of Israel will always be with them in Jesus Name. Amen!

Our children will never be stranded in life, they are covered by the four cardinal blessings. The blessings of the heavens, the blessings of the deepest ocean and the blessings of the womb, and breast.

*Lord, we thank You for You have heard and answered us in Jesus Name. Amen!

Meditation/Action Plan

1.____

2.____

3.____

4.____

5.____

Day

Insert your children's names

Daniel 6:3 (BBE Version)
Then this Daniel did his work better than the chief rulers and the captains, because there was a special spirit in him, and it was the king's purpose to put him over all the kingdom.

Prayers

You are chosen and preferred above all because you have an excellent spirit.

God will grant our children favor and compassion before princes and kings or decision-makers in Jesus Name. Amen!

God will be with our children and grant them success in everything in Jesus Name. Amen!

Our children will prosper in whatever is handed over to them to do in school, at work, and in the community in Jesus Name. Amen!

Our children shall be sought after by their institutions, organizations, and society in Jesus Name. Amen!

Our children shall develop the spirit of excellence, and this shall set them apart from others in Jesus Name. Amen!

Our children will find favor before God and man so that the decisions of man will favor them in Jesus Name. Amen!

The favor card will always work for our children, anytime they present it in Jesus Name. Amen!

If there is one slot left for any application made by our children, it shall be reserved for them in Jesus Name. Amen!

**Lord, we thank You for You have heard and answered us in Jesus Name. Amen!*

Meditation/Action Plan

1.____

____

____

____

2.____

____

____

____

3.____

____

____

____

4.____

____

____

____

5.____

____

____

____

Day

22

Insert your children's names

Matthew 5:14 (BBE Version)
You are the light of the world. A town put on a hill may be seen by all.

Matthew 5:14 (Easy English) You are like the light that everybody needs in this world. If people build a city on a hill, then other people can see it easily.

Prayers

You are a light to the world, and a city set upon the hill cannot be hidden.

Our children will receive the ability to shine the light in them in Jesus Name. Amen!

The world is in darkness and needs light, and our children will be the light that will shine in the dark in Jesus Name. Amen!

Every light has its coverage radius, and our children will find the radius that their light will cover in Jesus Name (Area of impact). Amen!

The world will recognize the light in them, and they will search for them to illuminate their darkness in Jesus Name. Amen!

No one can dull the light from the sun, and no one can dull the shine of our children in Jesus Name. Amen!

Our children are positioned prominently like a city on the hill so they cannot be hidden, and all will come to see and feel their impact in Jesus Name. Amen!

Our children are light, therefore they cannot dwell in darkness in Jesus Name. Amen!

Darkness cannot comprehend light therefore our children will never be overwhelmed by darkness in Jesus Name. Amen!

**Lord, we thank You for You have heard and answered us in Jesus Name. Amen!*

Meditation/Action Plan

1.____

____

____

____

2.____

____

____

____

3.____

____

____

____

4.____

____

____

____

5.____

____

____

____

Day

Insert your Children's Names

Psalm 125:3 BBE
For the rod of sinners will not be resting on the heritage of the upright; so that the upright may not put out their hands to evil.

Prayers

Every evil around our children either on social media or physical association will not rest on them, so they will not fall prey to it in Jesus Name. Amen!

Our children will not be baptised into evil and they will be far from evil works in Jesus Name. Amen!

We pray that wrong association that will lead to regret in life will not locate our children in the mighty Name of Jesus. Amen!

The authority or evil pronunciation of the enemy shall not rest upon our children in Jesus Name. Amen!

Our children will not fall prey to the manipulation of the evil one in Jesus Name. Amen!

Our children will not engage in activities of darkness no matter how enticing it is packaged in Jesus Name. Amen!

Evil will never be packaged as good by deceitful friends for our children in Jesus Name. Amen!

We pray that God will not allow the oppression of the wicked to lead our children, to dip their hands into evil deeds in Jesus Name. Amen!

Our children will never fall into the spell of the evil one in Jesus Name. Amen!

*Lord we thank You for You have heard and answered us in Jesus Name. **Amen!**

Meditation/Action Plan

1.____

____

____

____

2.____

____

____

____

3.____

____

____

____

4.____

____

____

____

5.____

____

____

____

Day

Insert your children's names

Deuteronomy 31:6
(Easy English) Be strong and be brave! Do not be afraid of them, because the LORD your God goes with you. He will never leave you nor forget you.'

Isaiah 43:19 ISV
Watch! I'm about to carry out something new! And now it's springing up— don't you recognize it? I'm making a way in the wilderness and paths in the desert.

Prayers

They will never be stranded in life, and they will always know what to do in Jesus Name. Amen!

Our Children will be strong and courageous in the face of adversities in Jesus Name. Amen!

Our children will not jump the gun, and they will wait for the Lord to always go before them so that they will never be afraid in Jesus Name. Amen!

We cast away from our children every spirit of fear that stifles and cripples progress in Jesus Name. Amen!

In times of adversities, our children will always have a sense of security as they remember that God has declared in His word, that He will never leave nor forget them. This confidence shall give them the strength to overcome in Jesus Name. Amen!

Our children shall enter into a new dimension of God in every area of their lives in this season in Jesus Name. Amen!

Sometimes in life, God uses adversities to bring something new into our lives, and most people do not recognize it. We pray that our children will have spiritual eyes that would recognize new seasons in their lives in Jesus Name. Amen!

God will always make a way during tough times for our children, and they will never lose sight of God in Jesus Name. Amen!

Our children shall be victorious in Christ over every battle of life, and no evil will overcome them in Jesus Name. Amen!

We pray for God to deliver us from every manipulation of the evil one and his cohorts, they shall not succeed in their evil enterprise in Jesus Name. Amen!

*Lord, we thank You for You have heard and answered our prayers over our children in Jesus Name. **Amen!**

Meditation/Action Plan

1._______________________________________
____
____
____

2._______________________________________
____
____
____

3._______________________________________
____
____
____

4._______________________________________
____
____
____

5._______________________________________
____
____
____

Day

Insert your children's Names

Psalm 144:12 NET
Then our sons will be like plants that quickly grow to full size. Our daughters will be like corner pillars carved like those in a palace.

Prayers

Our sons will be strong, and our daughters will grow to be strong pillars of support in places of honor in Jesus Name. Amen!

Strong plants produce fruits, and they are fruitful and support all that need nourishment around them; the birds, butterflies, and the human that feed on the fruit. The plants are strong enough to sustain all that depend on them, we pray that our sons will be productive in every season of their lives and support those that rely on them in Jesus Name. Amen!

Our daughters are like the corner pillars of the palace they do not only adorn the palace but support it firmly; without the corner pillars, the palace cannot stand the test of time. Our daughters will be women of substance with intrinsic values that will help them build lasting structures in Jesus Name. Amen!

Women can function effectively and fulfil their roles when they are not under undue stress; our sons will develop the capacity to provide a less stressful environment for their future wives to operate in Jesus Name. Amen!

Everyone, both men and women, have their responsibilities cut out for them. The men should be strong to support the family structure through clear leadership and financial stability. We pray that our sons' strength will never wane no matter the circumstances, and they will be able to support their families at all times in Jesus Name. Amen!

A woman should be as beautiful inside out, but most importantly, as firm and supportive as the corner pillars. When too much pressure (undue pressure) is placed on the corner pillars, the structure might collapse. Our daughters will not experience the coercion that would make their pillars collapse in Jesus Name. Amen!

We pray fervently for our sons to grow up with the capacity to support the pillars that would hold their structures in place and not subject them to undue stress in Jesus Name. Amen!

Likewise, we pray that our daughters will grow with the character and strength of the corner pillars. They will build capacity to supports a beautiful structure in Jesus Name. Amen!

Our children will not marry irresponsible spouses, but they will choose wisely with the help of the spirit of God directing them, and they will not choose on a superficial level in Jesus Name. Amen!

The ability to choose the right spouse does not exempt any marriage from turbulence, but it opens one up to receive the grace and strength to weather through it. So we pray for our children to receive the grace and resilience for whatever challenges may be associated with the spouse of God's choice for them in Jesus Name. Amen!

Lord, we thank You for You have heard and answered us in Jesus Name. **Amen!*

Meditation/Action Plan

1.____
____
____
____

2.____
____
____
____

3.____
____
____
____

4.____
____
____
____

5.____
____
____
____

Day

26

Insert your children's Names

Gen 2:18 ISV
Later, the LORD God said, "It is not good for the man to be alone. I will make the woman to be an authority corresponding to him."

Eph 5:25 ISV
Husbands, love your wives as the Messiah loved the church and gave Himself for it,

Prayers

God will provide the right spouses for our children when the time comes, and for those who are married, God will perfect their marriages in Jesus Name. Amen!

God will make our daughters strong and powerful to provide support for their future husbands in Jesus Name. Amen!

God will provide the woman who would be the right support for our sons in Jesus Name. Amen!

The love of Christ for the church is selfless, so we pray

that our daughters will find husbands who would love them and care for them like Christ loves the church in Jesus Name. Amen!

Our children will not be unequally yoked in marriage with unbelievers in Jesus Name. Amen!

Our children will not marry spouses that would directly or indirectly destroy them, and they will not wed a mismatch in Jesus Name. Amen!

Some women marry, and they become emotional wreck after some years. Our daughters will never fall victim to men that would abuse their emotions in Jesus Name. Amen!

Our sons will not marry women that are wicked and whose intent is to use and destroy them, and they will not be physically or emotionally tortured in Jesus Name. Amen!

Couples who are married sometimes still feel lonely; our children will not embrace loneliness in marriage, and they will marry spouses who would accept them totally (weaknesses and strength) in Jesus Name. Amen!

Our children and their spouses will be faithful to each other, there shall be no communication gap in their relationship, and the spirit of infidelity shall be far from them in Jesus Name. Amen!

Our children will marry their friend, and they will never marry their enemy in Jesus Name. Amen!

*Lord, we thank You for You have heard and answered us in Jesus Name. **Amen!**

Meditation/Action Plan

1.____

2.____

3.____

4.____

5.____

Day

Insert your children's Names

Exodus 14:13 BBE
But Moses said, keep where you are and have no fear; now you will see the salvation of the Lord which He will give you today; for the Egyptians whom you see today you will never see again.

Prayers

Our children shall always be calm in the face of danger because they shall see the salvation of God in Jesus Name. Amen!

We pray for children who are involved in pornography, cults, and other criminal activities that they will experience the salvation of God in Jesus Name. Amen!

We pray that our children will not be drawn into the circle and cycle of addiction of whatever kind in Jesus Name. Amen!

Our daughters will not be lured into prostitution of any kind in the Name of Jesus. Amen!

Our children will not Fall into the den of drug addicts or substance abusers in Jesus Name. Amen!

We pray that children and teenagers (the youth) all around us who have been led into gangs, criminal activities, and prostitution will see the saving grace of God and deliverance in Jesus Name. Amen!

We Pray that they will have an open heart to hear God, at this time, and that the chains over their lives will be broken in Jesus Name. Amen!

We pray that God will send mentors and role models who will help them make headway and remain focused in Jesus Name. Amen!

We pray that our children will never bring reproach on themselves and to us; God will be a shield around them, and every enemy of their souls shall be destroyed in Jesus Name. Amen!

Every unfriendly friend whose mission is to pull them into their evil world will be completely disengaged from them forever in Jesus Name. Amen!

Lord, we thank You for You have heard and answered us in Jesus Name. **Amen!*

Meditation/Action Plan

1.____
____
____
____

2.____
____
____
____

3.____
____
____
____

4.____
____
____
____

5.____
____
____
____

Day

Insert your children's Names

Luke 2:52 NET
And Jesus increased in wisdom and in stature, and in favour with God and with people.

Prayers

Our children will grow in God's wisdom in Jesus Name. Amen!

Divine wisdom is different from worldly wisdom; it is unquestionable because it is pure and explicit. We pray for this kind of sagacity for our children throughout their lives in Jesus Name. Amen!

We pray that our children will grow up gracefully, with well-built and nurtured bodies, their faculties growing in the right proportion to match their purpose on earth in Jesus Name. Amen!

We pray that our children would realize that their bodies are the temple of the Holy Ghost, and they should protect and take care of it by feeding it with the right food and nourishment in Jesus Name. Amen!

We pray that our children will not abuse their bodies in

any way but would preserve it holy for the use of their creator in Jesus Name. Amen!

I realize that someone can be highly knowledgeable but unable to apply the knowledge, and they are literate but not wise. We pray that our children will develop the capacity to apply the knowledge acquired, they will not be foolish in life, they will make the right decisions in Jesus Name. Amen!

We pray that our children will exhibit the love of Christ to humanity, and they will serve God by showing kindness to others around them in Jesus Name. Amen!

We pray that our children will develop a heart big enough to show real compassion to all of their fellowmen in Jesus Name. Amen!

We pray that our children will find favor before man, and that favor will surround them everywhere they go in Jesus Name. Amen!

We pray that our children will forever grow in the favor of God in all areas of their lives in Jesus Name. Amen!

**Lord, we thank You for You have heard and answered us in Jesus Name. Amen!*

Meditation/Action Plan

1.

2.

3.

4.

5.

Day

29

Insert your children's Names

Genesis 12:3 BBE
To them who are good to you will I give blessing, and on him who does you wrong will I put My curse: and you will become a name of blessing to all the families of the earth.

Prayers

Our children will be a blessing to the world in Jesus Name. *Amen!*

Our children are blessed and favored; people will be good to them in Jesus Name. Amen!

Our children's lives will attract blessings, and those who bless them will be blessed in Jesus Name. Amen!

In the Name of Jesus, our children cannot be cursed. Anyone who curses them without reason is cursed.

Our children bear the mark of Christ upon their lives; no one troubles them in Jesus Name. Amen!

Presently Bill Gates is a name of blessings to families of the earth, and he is solving poverty issues for the poorest countries in the world, Imagine how much more our children can do, who have the power of the Holy Spirit of God. We pray that our children will become the name of blessings to all the families of the earth in Jesus Name. *Amen!*

Through our children, our salvation and solutions shall be brought to the families of the world in Jesus Name. *Amen!*

Through our children, shall rise world leaders and great philanthropists the world has never seen in Jesus Name. *Amen!*

Our children shall wake up to the power of their inheritance in Christ. They will walk in the power of the blessings of God upon their lives in the Name of Jesus. *Amen!*

* Lord, we thank You for You have heard and answered us in Jesus Name. *Amen!*

Meditation/Action Plan

1.____
____
____
____

2.____
____
____
____

3.____
____
____
____

4.____
____
____
____

5.____
____
____
____

Day

Insert your children's names

Isaiah 60:1 (Easy English)
Stand up and shine! Do that because your light has come! And the glory of the LORD has risen over you.

Sometimes when we are down, we do not understand why we need to stand and shine, we do not fathom that light shines and disperse darkness, we owe it to ourselves to stand, we owe it to God to shine so we can disperse darkness for others to see and be delivered. So this Scripture is a command, not a mere statement or an instruction. We pray today that our children will walk in the revelation of Isaiah 60:1. They will always arise and shine no matter the circumstance in Jesus Name. Amen!

Prayers

The sunlight shines far and wide to cover areas around it. Our children will shine bright in every area of their lives in Jesus Name. Amen!

A loser is not the person that fails but the person who fails to rise when they fall. Our children will arise from *any form of failure and shine in Jesus Name. **Amen!***

*We get so distracted with what we have failed at and sometimes miss when the spotlight of God is on us as it was on the sons of Issachar, our children will be aware of the signs of the spotlight of God upon them so they arise and shine in the Name of Jesus. **Amen!***

*When the glory of God is upon someone, then enemies cannot withstand or stop them. The glory of the Lord has risen upon our children, and the enemy cannot dim their glory in Jesus Name. **Amen!***

*The difficult step to take in the time of adversity is to stand up and step out; to shine, the Sun has to overcome the greatest darkness called midnight to begin the journey of rising at dawn. Our children will never lack the strength to stand up and shine when the need arises in Jesus Name. **Amen!***

*We pray for children going through a bout of depression, and we declare to their spirit the strength to stand up and shine because their light has come in the Name of Jesus. **Amen!***

We pray for our Grandchildren and declare they shall arise and shine for the glory of God shall rise upon them in Jesus Name. Amen!

We pray for ourselves as Moms; that we will not be obstacles to the rising and shining of our children; through behavioral defect, lack of discipline, or by overindulging of our children in Jesus Name. Amen!

**Thank You, Lord, for answering our prayer all through these 30 days; we are so grateful for Your grace, mercy, and Strength. Amen! Amen!! Amen!!!*

Meditation/Action Plan

1.

2.

3.

4.

5.

Congratulations!!! Moms, you did it! Well done and great job!

You can use this Prayer Guide repeatedly every Month or for a 30 Day intensive prayer and fasting session for your children.

As Mothers, we must never stop praying for our children; it is a spiritual investment into their future.

www.ingramcontent.com/pod-product-compliance
Lightning Source LLC
Chambersburg PA
CBHW030317160726
47992CB00005B/2040